THE BEST
KEY WEST
TRIVIA
BOOK EVER

DAVID L SLOAN

PHANTOM PRESS
KEYWEST

For use of information contained as source material, credit: David L. Sloan, author, The Best Key West Trivia Book Ever.

Special thanks to Dorothy Drennen, Michael Crisp, Heather-May Potter & Brad Bertelli.

Inquiries: david@phantompress.com

ISBN: **978-0-9831671-2-9**

HOW TO PLAY

HAVE FUN

If you remember all of the information in this book, you will know more about Key West than most locals. Some questions are hard and some are easy. The rest are somewhere in between. Don't feel bad if you don't know the answers. Soak in the knowledge and have fun.

THE RULES

The book has 50 quizzes about Key West and the Florida Keys. Each quiz has 10 questions about a specific topic. Write down your answers on a separate sheet of paper, then turn the page to see the correct answers and tally up your score.

SCORING

Each correct answer is worth 1 point. A perfect score for any quiz is 10 points. Each answer page has a scoring area at the bottom where you can write your name, score for that quiz, and grand total. Once you complete all of the quizzes we'll tell you how smart you are when it comes to Key West.

NUMBER OF PLAYERS

There is no limit to how many people can play. We've included space for 4 people on the scoring sheet. After that you can buy another book, scribble in the margins or stop keeping score and pretend you got most of them right.

SHARING

Share the quiz questions with family and friends. Pass the book on to someone you think will enjoy it. If you loved the book, share with a review on Amazon. If you didn't love it, share with me so I can make it better. My e-mail is david@phantompress.com. Enjoy.

CATEGORIES

1. **KEY WEST 101**
2. **MALLORY SQUARE**
3. **EARLY DAYS**
4. **PIRACY & TREASURE**
5. **SOUTHERNMOST POINT**
6. **WRECKING**
7. **PRESIDENTS**
8. **IN SONG**
9. **TURTLE & SHRIMP**
10. **ERNEST HEMINGWAY**
11. **HURRICANES**
12. **BURIAL GROUNDS**
13. **CIGARS**
14. **FORTS**
15. **TV SHOWS**
16. **RESTAURANT NAMES**
17. **BLACK HISTORY**
18. **LITERARY**
19. **THE CONCH REPUBLIC**
20. **PARANORMAL**
21. **FAMOUS RESIDENTS**
22. **ARCHITECTURE**
23. **KEY LIME PIE**
24. **BAR NAMES**
25. **CONCHS & SPONGES**

CATEGORIES

THE BEST
KEY WEST
TRIVIA
BOOK EVER

DAVID L SLOAN

QUIZ #1
KEY WEST 101

1. How did Key West get its name?

2. What geographical claim makes Key West unique?

3. How large is Key West according to most sources?

4. How far is Key West from Cuba?

5. Which two bodies of water surround Key West?

6. What county is Key West a part of?

7. What is Key West's primary zip code?

8. What term is used to describe someone born in Key West?

9. What is Key West's maximum elevation?

10. What road connects Key West to the mainland?

QUIZ #1
ANSWERS

1. The name Key West comes from the Spanish "*Cayo Hueso*" meaning "*bone key*" or "*island of bones.*"

2. Key West is the southernmost city in the continental United States.

3. Most sources claim that Key West is 2 miles wide by 4 miles long. Different parameters are used for measurement by different sources, but the Chamber of Commerce asserts that Key West is roughly 1.5 miles wide by 4 miles long.

4. 90 miles is the claim, but it is actually 103 miles.

5. The Atlantic Ocean and the Gulf of Mexico

6. Monroe County

7. 33040

8. Conch

9. About 18 feet at Solares Hill

10. US1, also known as the Overseas Highway

NAME	SCORE	GRAND TOTAL
_____	_____	_____
_____	_____	_____
_____	_____	_____
_____	_____	_____

QUIZ #2
MALLORY SQUARE

1. What is the name of the primary event that draws people to Mallory Square?

2. Who is Mallory Square named after?

3. Mallory Square had a former name. What was it?

4. Who is credited with starting the tradition of applauding sunset at Mallory Square?

5. What organization manages the nightly celebration at Mallory Square?

6. In what decade did the contemporary incarnation of watching sunset at Mallory Square begin?

7. What group of people started the tradition of gathering at Mallory Square each evening?

8. What did this group of people take to enhance the Mallory Square sunset experience?

9. What treat did Marilyn Kellner sell at Mallory Square?

10. What threatened to block the view of sunset before artists and performers protested?

QUIZ #2
ANSWERS

1. Sunset Celebration

2. Florida Senator Stephen Russell Mallory (1812-1873)

3. Tift's Wharf, after wrecker and merchant Asa Tift

4. Tennessee Williams

5. The Key West Cultural Preservation Society, Inc.

6. The 1960s

7. Gypsies or Freaks

8. LSD

9. Cookies

10. Cruise ships

9

NAME	SCORE	GRAND TOTAL
_____	_____	_____
_____	_____	_____
_____	_____	_____
_____	_____	_____

QUIZ #3
EARLY DAYS

1. What country was the first to claim Key West as part of its territory?

2. In what year did Juan Pablo Salas acquire Key West as part of a land grant?

3. How many times did Juan Pablo Salas sell Key West?

4. In what year was the City of Key West incorporated?

5. What did Navy Lt. Commandant Matthew Perry plant in Key West on March 25, 1822?

6. What alternate name did Matthew Perry assign to Key West?

7. What was the name of Key West's first newspaper?

8. What product did Key West start producing in 1830 for food preservation?

9. What was the population of Key West in 1830?

10. Key West's early settlers were primarily from what region?

QUIZ #3
ANSWERS

1. Spain

2. 1815

3. Two -- to John Simonton and John Geddes.

4. 1828

5. The United States flag

6. Thompson's Island

7. *The Register*

8. Salt

9. 517

10. New England

NAME	SCORE	GRAND TOTAL
_____	_____	_____
_____	_____	_____
_____	_____	_____
_____	_____	_____

QUIZ #4
PIRACY & TREASURE

1. On what street in Key West is the "Pirate's Well" located?

2. What bar has a tree in it where legend claims pirates were hanged?

3. What is the name of the Commodore who was assigned to Key West to eradicate piracy?

4. What pirate is said to have escaped a slave ship before setting up shop in the Florida Keys?

5. What influential ocean current brought ships close to the Florida Keys, making the Keys an ideal location for pirates?

6. What caused eight ships of the Spanish Treasure Fleet to sink in 1622?

7. What shipwreck from the 1622 fleet did Mel Fisher discover in 1985?

8. What did divers call this ship's sandy wreckage site?

9. What prized treasures discovered by Mel Fisher came from the Muzo Mine in Columbia?

10. What did Mel Fisher raise before becoming a treasure hunter?

QUIZ #4
ANSWERS

1. Caroline

2. Captain Tony's

3. Commodore David Porter

4. Black Caesar

5. The Gulf Stream

6. A hurricane

7. Nuestra Señora de Atocha

8. The Bank of Spain

9. Emeralds

10. Chickens

NAME	SCORE	GRAND TOTAL
_____	_____	_____
_____	_____	_____
_____	_____	_____
_____	_____	_____

QUIZ #5
SOUTHERNMOST POINT

1.   In what year did the buoy marker first appear?

2.   What was the marker originally called in invitations to its dedication?

3.   Who came up with the idea for Southernmost Point marker?

4.   What type of buoy is the Southernmost Point marker modeled after?

5.   How much does the Southernmost Point marker weigh?

6.   How much did the original Southernmost Point marker cost to build?

7.   What president was officially invited to the dedication of the Southernmost Point?

8.   Where did some residents try to get the Southernmost Point marker relocated to in 1997?

9.   Is the marker located on the real southernmost point?

10. What was located near the Southernmost Point but was relocated after the Great Havana Hurricane of 1846?

QUIZ #5
ANSWERS

1. 1983

2. The Southernmost Geographical Monument

3. City administrative aide C.W. "Billy" Pinder

4. A Nun Buoy

5. 9.8 tons. It is made of concrete.

6. $902.17

7. President Ronald Reagan. He did not attend.

8. The end of Duval Street

9. No. A more southernmost point exists on Navy property.

10. A burial ground

NAME	SCORE	GRAND TOTAL
_____	_____	_____
_____	_____	_____
_____	_____	_____
_____	_____	_____

QUIZ #6
WRECKING

1. Wrecking refers to salvaging what?

2. Who were the first people to salvage ships in the Florida Keys?

3. What Act was passed in 1825 to prevent the spoils of shipwrecks within U.S. jurisdiction from being carried to foreign ports?

4. What famous wrecker lived in the home now known as the Audubon House?

5. How many rules of wrecking did the courts employ?

6. What title was given to the first person to arrive at a wreck?

7. What beverage was a wrecked ship carrying when the courts decreed "no additional salvage fees" because of the amount of the beverage consumed during the salvage?

8. What movie starring John Wayne dramatized the wrecking industry?

9. What innovation ushered in the end of the wrecking era?

10. In what year did the Wrecking License Bureau close?

QUIZ #6
ANSWERS

1. Ships that have wrecked on the reef or become stranded

2. Native Americans

3. The Federal Wrecking Act

4. John Geiger

5. 13

6. Wrecking master

7. Beer

8. *Reap the Wild Wind*

9. The lighthouse

10. 1921

NAME	SCORE	GRAND TOTAL
_____	_____	_____
_____	_____	_____
_____	_____	_____
_____	_____	_____

QUIZ #7
PRESIDENTS

1. What is the name of the former presidential home in Key West's Truman Annex?

2. What president resided in Key West for 175 days of his term?

3. What does the sign on President Truman's Key West desk say?

4. What president visited Key West for 12 days at the end of 1955 and beginning of 1956 while recovering from a heart attack?

5. Who was the first president to visit Key West?

6. What former peanut farmer and former president visited Key West in 1996 and 2007?

7. What inventor perfected 41 underwater weapons during his six-month stay at the Little White House?

8. The Key West Agreement of 1948 set parameters for the creation of what department?

9. What street was renamed "Truman Avenue" in honor of President Truman?

10. What president visited Key West in 1962 immediately following the Cuban Missile Crisis?

QUIZ #7
ANSWERS

1. The Little White House

2. President Harry S. Truman

3. The Buck Stops Here

4. President Dwight D. Eisenhower

5. Ulysses S. Grant (1880)

6. President Jimmy E. Carter

7. Thomas Edison

8. Department of Defense

9. Division Street

10. President John F. Kennedy

NAME   **SCORE**   **GRAND TOTAL**

_____   _____   _____

_____   _____   _____

_____   _____   _____

_____   _____   _____

QUIZ #8
IN SONG

1. What dessert created in Key West does Kenny Chesney claim is "not too tart, not too sweet?"

2. What group of macho men sang the lyric, "I'm heading for Key West, the key to happiness?"

3. What Key West resident wrote *A Boy Named Sue* and *The Great Conch Train Robbery*?

4. Harry Connick Jr. sang that he rode a roller coaster to Key West. Where did he ride it from?

5. What country music star joins Jimmy Buffett in the song *Conky Tonkin'*?

6. What band refers to Key West as a "world party" in their song *Keep This Party Going*?

7. What bridge "connected on Marathon shore" and was the "gateway to Key West" in a David Allan Coe song?

8. Which Smashing Pumpkins member named a side project album after a local Catholic church?

9. What band did local celebrity Paul Cotton used to be a member of?

10. What Grammy Award winning artist wrote *Key West Intermezzo (I Saw You First)*?

QUIZ #8
ANSWERS

1. Key Lime Pie

2. The Village People

3. Shel Silverstein

4. *Coney Island (You Didn't Know Me When)*

5. Clint Black

6. B-52's

7. *Seven Mile Bridge*

8. Billy Corgan with Zwan's *Mary Star of the Sea*

9. Poco

10. John Mellencamp

NAME   **SCORE**   **GRAND TOTAL**

_____ _____ _____

_____ _____ _____

_____ _____ _____

_____ _____ _____

QUIZ #9
TURTLES & SHRIMP

1. What term was used to describe the color and value of shrimp found off the waters of Key West?

2. What islands were the fertile shrimp beds found closest to?

3. Where was Key West's shrimp fleet based?

4. What did workers remove from the shrimp before they were packed in ice and shipped?

5. Where did the Key West shrimp fleet relocate as their numbers started to dwindle?

6. What islands were named for their lack of water and abundance of turtles?

7. What term describes the pens where captured turtles were kept? A restaurant of the same name sits on a site where they were located.

8. The fat of the green turtle was highly desired as a base for what delicacy?

9. When did the first turtle cannery open in Key West?

10. What lead to the decline of the turtle industry?

QUIZ #9
ANSWERS

1. Pink Gold

2. The Dry Tortugas

3. The Key West Bight or Historic Seaport

4. Their heads

5. Stock Island

6. The Dry Tortugas

7. Turtle Kraals

8. Soup

9. 1857

10. Overfishing

NAME	SCORE	GRAND TOTAL
_____	_____	_____
_____	_____	_____
_____	_____	_____
_____	_____	_____

QUIZ #10
ERNEST HEMINGWAY

1.   What is the name of Ernest Hemingway's first Key West residence?

2.   What was the name of the hotel where the Hemingways stayed for two years upon arriving in Key West?

3.   What year did Hemingway arrive in Key West?

4.   Who built the house Hemingway would call home at 907 Whitehead Street?

5.   What term is used to describe cats like those at the Hemingway Home with six or more toes on one foot?

6.   What was the nickname of Hemingway's friend and bar owner, Joe Russell?

7.   What is the title of the book Hemingway wrote about a Key West sea captain?

8.   What wife did Hemingway live with in Key West?

9.   What is the name of Hemingway's boat?

10. In what year did Hemingway leave Key West and where did he move?

QUIZ #10
ANSWERS

1. Casa Antigua

2. Trev-Mor Hotel

3. 1928

4. Asa Tift

5. Polydactyl

6. Sloppy Joe

7. To Have and Have Not

8. Pauline Pfeiffer Hemingway

9. Pilar

10. 1939, Cuba

NAME	SCORE	GRAND TOTAL
_____	_____	_____
_____	_____	_____
_____	_____	_____
_____	_____	_____

QUIZ #11
HURRICANES

1. What hurricane destroyed the original Key West Lighthouse?

2. What connection to the mainland was wiped out by a hurricane in 1935?

3. On what weekend did the 1935 hurricane strike the Keys?

4. How did railroad workers protect their equipment when the 1909 hurricane arrived?

5. Where is Key West's "Hurricane Grotto" located?

6. The "Hurricane Grotto" is dedicated to whom?

7. What nun designed the grotto after witnessing three destructive hurricanes in Key West?

8. What famous writer's public outrage spurred an investigation after his fellow veterans were prevented from escaping the 1935 hurricane?

9. What neighboring key did the eye of Hurricane Irma strike in 2017?

10. What iconic Sugarloaf tower was brought down by Hurricane Irma?

QUIZ #11
ANSWERS

1. The Great Havana Hurricane of 1846

2. The Overseas Railroad

3. Labor Day

4. They intentionally sank it

5. The Basilica of Saint Mary Star of the Sea

6. Our Lady of Lourdes

7. Sister Louis Gabriel

8. Ernest Hemingway

9. Cudjoe Key

10. Perky Bat Tower

NAME	SCORE	GRAND TOTAL
_____	_____	_____
_____	_____	_____
_____	_____	_____
_____	_____	_____

QUIZ #12
BURIAL GROUNDS

1. What aspect of the Key West Cemetery's location made it desirable in 1847?

2. What happened to the occupants of an earlier burial ground on the south side of the island?

3. What humorous epitaph is credited to a supposed hypochondriac?

4. The Key West Cemetery features a monument to the soldiers of what ship that exploded in Havana Harbor after leaving Key West in 1898?

5. What animals are buried in the Otto family plot of the Key West Cemetery?

6. What resident of the Key West Cemetery used to box with Ernest Hemingway?

7. What bar contains the gravestone of Elvira?

8. What three slave ships carried those now buried in the African Cemetery at Higgs Beach?

9. Behind which church is the grave of Thomas Jefferson's descendent, Captain Thomas Mann Randolph?

10. The bar in which drinking hole contains the cremains of some of their most loyal customers?

QUIZ #12
ANSWERS

1.   High elevation

2.   They were washed away in a hurricane

3.   I Told You I Was Sick

4.   USS Maine

5.   Three Yorkshire Terriers and one Key Deer

6.   Kermit "Shine" Forbes

7.   Captain Tony's Saloon

8.   The Wildfire, the William, and the Bogota

9.   Saint Paul's Episcopal Church

10. The Chart Room

NAME   **SCORE**   **GRAND TOTAL**

_____   _____   _____

_____   _____   _____

_____   _____   _____

_____   _____   _____

QUIZ #13
CIGARS

1. The production of hand rolled cigars was Key West's largest industry in which two centuries?

2. What unofficial title did Key West earn by producing one hundred million cigars a year?

3. What were cigar factories operated from small or modest wooden houses called?

4. Why are the windows on the north side of many cigar factories larger than those on the south side?

5. What was the name of the successful industrial community Edward Gato built around his cigar factory?

6. What country sold Cuban tobacco to Key West to help fund their troops?

7. The Great Fire of what year destroyed 18 major cigar factories?

8. After the Great Fire, which Florida city lured cigar factories to them with promises of tax breaks?

9. What cigar factory employee kept cigar factory workers entertained?

10. What was the biggest threat to cigar production in Key West, apart from fire?

QUIZ #13
ANSWERS

1. 19th and early 20th

2. Cigar Capital of the World

3. Buckeyes

4. To enhance the breeze

5. Gatoville

6. Spain

7. 1886

8. Tampa

9. The lector (reader) who read books aloud

10. Worker strikes

NAME	SCORE	GRAND TOTAL
_____	_____	_____
_____	_____	_____
_____	_____	_____
_____	_____	_____

QUIZ #14
FORTS

1. How many forts exist in Key West?

2. What fort's construction started as part of a government plan to eradicate piracy?

3. What fort is home to Robert the Doll?

4. What fort is home to the Key West Garden Club?

5. What term is used to describe a fort with an inner tower or citadel and thick outer walls?

6. What animals were brought in to control vegetation at Battery Seminole?

7. What fort is located about 70 miles west of Key West in the Dry Tortugas?

8. Who was held at this Dry Tortugas fort after assisting the man who shot President Lincoln?

9. In what Key West neighborhood is Fort Street located?

10. Who controlled Fort Zachary Taylor during the Civil War?

QUIZ #14
ANSWERS

1. Three

2. Fort Zachary Taylor

3. Fort East Martello

4. West Martello Tower

5. Martello

6. Goats

7. Fort Jefferson

8. Samuel Mudd

9. Bahama Village

10. The Union

NAME	SCORE	GRAND TOTAL
_____	_____	_____
_____	_____	_____
_____	_____	_____
_____	_____	_____

QUIZ #15
TV SHOWS

1. Marcus Lemonis became involved with what dessert company on his TV show *The Profit*?

2. On what key was *The Real World: Key West* house located?

3. Who played the main character, Seamus O'Neill, in the 1993 TV series *Key West*?

4. What Netflix psychological thriller filmed in the Florida Keys revolved around the Rayburn family?

5. CNN regularly features footage of what Key West New Year's Eve event?

6. What TV show featured Jack Osbourne searching for ghosts in the Dry Tortugas?

7. The second season cast of MTV's *Road Rules* met in front of what famous Key West landmark?

8. What charming Bravo reality show celebrated Cameran's birthday here in the episode: *A Tribe Called Key West?*

9. On what show did Guy Fieri visit Garbo's Grill, D.J.'s Clam Shack, and Bad Boy Burrito?

10. Local DJ James Cooper sent his wife Joanna to live with a husband obsessed with entering sweepstakes. What reality show was this for?

QUIZ #15
ANSWERS

1. The Key West Key Lime Pie Co.

2. Key Haven

3. Fisher Stevens

4. *Bloodline*

5. A drag queen dropping in a giant shoe

6. *Haunted Highway*

7. The Southernmost Point

8. *Southern Charm*

9. *Diners, Drive-Ins and Dives*

10. *Wife Swap*

QUIZ #16
RESTAURANT NAMES

FILL IN THE BLANK TO COMPLETE THE LOCAL RESTAURANT NAME

1. Blue _____

2. First _____ Island Restaurant & Brewery

3. Only_____ Pizzeria

4. Smokin' _____

5. Banana _____

6. 2 _____

7. Tavern N _____

8. Garbo's _____

9. Cuban Coffee _____

10. Better Than _____

QUIZ #16
ANSWERS

1. Heaven or Macaw

2. Flight

3. Wood

4. Tuna

5. Cafe

6. Cents or Friends

7. Town

8. Grill

9. Queen

10. Sex

NAME	SCORE	GRAND TOTAL
_____	_____	_____
_____	_____	_____
_____	_____	_____
_____	_____	_____

QUIZ #17
BLACK HISTORY

1. What is the historically black neighborhood southwest of Whitehead Street called?

2. What slave ship found off the coast of Key West now has a plaque facing the African shore? The plaque honors the people the ship transported.

3. Manuel Cabeza was tarred and feathered by whom for dating a biracial Key West girl in 1921?

4. Where is the statue honoring black Union soldiers from Key West who fought in the Civil War?

5. What Key West park was named after the founding father of the Key West Junkanoos?

6. What did the City of Key West build in Bahama Village in 1946 when beaches were segregated?

7. What president issued an Executive Order against discrimination from his Key West home?

8. What black Deputy Sheriff was the first law officer in the Keys to be killed in the line of duty?

9. What illuminated vehicle was Mr. Chapman known for riding around Key West?

10. What Key West City Commissioner helped organize a march against a segregated skating rink when he was 13?

QUIZ #17
ANSWERS

1. Bahama Village

2. The Henrietta Marie

3. Ku Klux Klan

4. Bayview Park

5. Bill Butler Park

6. A swimming pool

7. Harry S Truman

8. Frank Adams

9. A tricycle

10. Clayton Lopez

NAME   **SCORE**   **GRAND TOTAL**

_____   _____   _____

_____   _____   _____

_____   _____   _____

_____   _____   _____

QUIZ #18
LITERARY

1. What author of *Are You There God? It's Me, Margaret* runs a bookstore in Key West?

2. On what Key West street did *Night of the Iguana* author Tennessee Williams reside?

3. 13 winners of which literary award have lived in Key West?

4. What poet broke his hand in two places when he punched Ernest Hemingway in the jaw?

5. What Lost Generation writer's advice prompted Ernest Hemingway to visit Key West?

6. What poet took the road less traveled and spent 16 consecutive winters in a Key West cottage on Caroline Street starting in 1945?

7. What author of this Trivia book also co-wrote *Quit Your Job and Move to Key West*?

8. What author wrote *The Giving Tree* and had his former home destroyed by a tree?

9. What author wrote *Ninety-Two In The Shade* and was tagged as the next Hemingway?

10. What two Key West authors have reached number one on both the fiction and non-fiction New York Times Best Seller lists?

QUIZ #18
ANSWERS

1. Judy Blume

2. Duncan Street

3. The Pulitzer Prize

4. Wallace Stevens

5. John Dos Passos

6. Robert Frost

7. David L. Sloan

8. Shel Silverstein

9. Tom McGuane

10. Ernest Hemingway and Jimmy Buffett

NAME   **SCORE**   **GRAND TOTAL**

_____   _____   _____

_____   _____   _____

_____   _____   _____

_____   _____   _____

QUIZ #19
THE CONCH REPUBLIC

1. The Conch Republic was formed in 1982 when Key West did what?

2. What action of the U.S. Border Patrol led to the formation of the Conch Republic?

3. What designation is given to the Conch Republic and other nations who claim to be independent but are not recognized by world governments?

4. What food product did the Conch Republic's Prime Minister use to declare war on the United States?

5. How much money did the Conch Republic request in foreign aid upon surrender?

6. The FBI believes that 9/11 hijacker Mohamed Atta purchased what from the Conch Republic?

7. What local treasure was named King of the Conch Republic?

8. What bridge did the Conch Republic claim after the government ruled it was not part of the U.S.?

9. Who was the Secretary General of the Conch Republic?

10. What race that takes place during the Conch Republic Independence Celebration features high heels instead of fast cars?

QUIZ #19
ANSWERS

1. Seceded from the Union

2. A roadblock

3. Micronation

4. Stale Cuban bread

5. One billion dollars

6. A souvenir passport

7. Mel Fisher

8. The Old Seven Mile Bridge

9. Peter Anderson

10. The Drag Race

NAME	SCORE	GRAND TOTAL
_____	_____	_____
_____	_____	_____
_____	_____	_____
_____	_____	_____

QUIZ #20
PARANORMAL

1. What type of doll is Robert the Doll?

2. Who believed the dead body of Elena Hoyos was communicating with him?

3. What bar is said to be haunted by "the blue lady"?

4. What guesthouse reports paranormal activity from Enriquetta, a mother who was removed from the home with her eight children?

5. What hotel is said to be haunted by the ghosts of people who jumped to their deaths?

6. What popular craft beer bar regularly receives dropped dimes from the ghost of Doctor Porter?

7. What bar is believed to be haunted by the wife of a former Pan Am pilot?

8. What Key West museum was home to the Mrs. Peck Doll? The doll was believed to be haunted and disappeared under mysterious circumstances.

9. What popular restaurant is Robert Curry said to haunt?

10. What type of animal is rumored to haunt Julia Street between Duval Street and Whitehead Street?

QUIZ #20
ANSWERS

1. Steiff

2. Carl Tanzler Von Cosel

3. Captain Tony's

4. Marrero's

5. La Concha Hotel

6. The Porch

7. First Flight Island Restaurant & Brewery

8. The Audubon House

9. The Hard Rock Cafe

10. A horse

NAME	SCORE	GRAND TOTAL
_____	_____	_____
_____	_____	_____
_____	_____	_____
_____	_____	_____

QUIZ #21
FAMOUS RESIDENTS

1. What actress starred in Top Gun and had a local restaurant named after her?

2. What world-famous fashion designer owned an octagon shaped house at 712 Eaton Street?

3. What *Breakfast at Tiffany's* novelist wintered in a doublewide trailer on the waterfront at the Pier House?

4. What NASCAR driver filmed a television show documenting the renovation of his house?

5. What founding member of the B-52's resides in Key West?

6. What *Fear and Loathing in Las Vegas* author offered "Gonzo Tours" when he lived in Key West?

7. What country singer briefly owned a home on Caroline Street?

8. What father of functional philosophy had a home on Greene Street?

9. What writer had a writing studio at his home he called "The Mad House"?

10. What New York Times Best Selling author and former president of the Philadelphia 76ers owns part of the Green Parrot?

QUIZ #21
ANSWERS

1. Kelly McGillis

2. Calvin Klein

3. Truman Capote

4. Dale Earnhardt Jr.

5. Keith Strickland

6. Hunter S. Thompson

7. Kenny Chesney

8. John Dewey

9. Tennessee Williams

10. Pat Croce

NAME	SCORE	GRAND TOTAL
_____	_____	_____
_____	_____	_____
_____	_____	_____
_____	_____	_____

QUIZ #22
ARCHITECTURE

1.   The home of John Bartlum was disassembled in which city before being shipped to Key West to be reassembled in the late 1840s?

2.   What are the small roof openings that improve air circulation called?

3.   Many carpenters who built Conch houses learned their trade building what?

4.   What firearm word describes a cottage with a side hall and three rooms, one behind another?

5.   Which regal style of architecture features towers and turrets?

6.   What durable, but now almost extinct, pine was used to build many houses in Key West?

7.   Metal shingle roofs were introduced to reduce the risk of what?

8.   What term describes the fanciful latticework adorning many Key West homes?

9.   What organization was founded in 1960 to promote the preservation and restoration of historically significant buildings?

10.   What device was used to collect rainwater before water was piped in from the mainland?

QUIZ #22
ANSWERS

1. Green Turtle Cay, Bahamas

2. Scuttles

3. Ships

4. Shotgun House

5. Queen Anne

6. Dade County Pine

7. Fire

8. Gingerbread

9. Old Island Restoration Foundation

10. A Cistern

NAME	SCORE	GRAND TOTAL
_____	_____	_____
_____	_____	_____
_____	_____	_____
_____	_____	_____

QUIZ #23
KEY LIME PIE

1. What color is Key lime pie supposed to be?

2. What are the three primary ingredients used to create the filling of Key lime pie?

3. Which seafaring residents of Key West are believed to have created the earliest version of Key lime pie?

4. In which historic inn is it said that Aunt Sally created the first Key lime pie?

5. What was Aunt Sally's real name?

6. What festival takes place each 4th of July weekend?

7. Who was granted a patent for sweetened condensed milk in 1856? He also invented the Lazy Susan.

8. Which Key lime pie ingredient was created to quell sexual urges?

9. What brand of biscuits did many Conchs used to use as a crust when they made Key lime pie?

10. What is the scientific name of the Key lime?

QUIZ #23
ANSWERS

1. Yellow

2. Eggs, sweetened condensed milk, and Key lime juice

3. Spongers

4. The Curry Mansion

5. Sarah Jane Lowe Curry

6. The Key Lime Festival

7. Gail Borden

8. The Graham Cracker

9. Uneeda Biscuits

10. Citrus Aurantiifolia

NAME	SCORE	GRAND TOTAL
_____	_____	_____
_____	_____	_____
_____	_____	_____
_____	_____	_____

QUIZ #24

BAR NAMES

FILL IN THE BLANK TO COMPLETE THE LOCAL BAR NAME

1. The Green _____

2. Don's _____

3. _____ Town

4. Garden of _____

5. Agave _____

6. Bobby's _____ Bar

7. The _____ & Whistle Bar

8. _____ Harry's

9. Shots and _____

10. Tattoos and _____

QUIZ #24
ANSWERS

1. Parrot

2. Place

3. Conch

4. Eden

5. 308

6. Monkey

7. Bull

8. Durty

9. Giggles

10. Scars

NAME	SCORE	GRAND TOTAL
_____	_____	_____
_____	_____	_____
_____	_____	_____
_____	_____	_____

QUIZ #25
CONCHS & SPONGES

1. What is the term for someone born in Key West?

2. What term describes someone who has lived in Key West for at least seven years?

3. What type of Conch can you become with a certificate from the County Mayor?

4. What are two terms of affection used by Conchs?

5. How did locals used to announce the birth of a new child?

6. In what decade were sponges first discovered in Key West?

7. What alternate name is given to spongers because of the three-tined forks they used to hook the sponges?

8. What did spongers use to see the sponges below the water?

9. Peaking with 1200 men working on 350 hook boats, how many tons of sponges did Key West produce annually?

10. The sponging industry declined, in part, when Greek immigrants arrived and harvested sponges in what?

QUIZ #25
ANSWERS

1. Conch

2. Freshwater Conch

3. Honorary

4. Cuzzy and Bubba

5. By placing a conch shell on a stick in the front yard

6. 1820s

7. Hookers

8. A glass bottom bucket

9. 2000 tons

10. Diving suits

NAME	SCORE	GRAND TOTAL
_____	_____	_____
_____	_____	_____
_____	_____	_____
_____	_____	_____

QUIZ #26
STREETS

1. What street is named for the man who purchased the island from Spanish artillery officer Juan Salas?

2. What street is named for a founding father of Key West who arrived after a shipwreck?

3. What four streets are named after U.S. Presidents?

4. Jimmy Buffett sang about a lady going crazy on what Key West street?

5. Name one of five streets named after siblings of John Whitehead.

6. What street is named for a founding father and former mayor? It is also home to most of the island's Key lime pie stores.

7. What street did Cubans dub *"Calle Iglesia"* (Church Street) due to all of the churches located there?

8. What street, named because it runs along the waterfront, was probably Key West's first street?

9. What street was named for a U.S. Senator and Andrew Jackson biographer?

10. What Old Town street was previously known as Chicken Bone Alley?

QUIZ #26
ANSWERS

1. Simonton Street

2. Whitehead Street

3. Truman Avenue, Kennedy Drive, Roosevelt Blvd., Eisenhower Drive

4. Caroline Street

5. Thomas, Emma, William, Margaret, Caroline

6. Greene Street

7. Eaton Street

8. Front Street

9. Eaton Street

10. Bahama Street

NAME	SCORE	GRAND TOTAL

QUIZ #27
KEYS LIGHTHOUSES

1. How many steps lead to the top of the Key West Lighthouse?

2. Why was lighthouse keeper Barbara Mabrity fired in 1864 after 32 years of service?

3. What happened to the Key West Lighthouse in 1969?

4. In what lighthouse did Rebecca Flaherty and five others die during the Great Havana Hurricane of 1846?

5. What lighthouse near the Matacumbe Keys was named for a U.S. Navy schooner that ran aground on the nearby reef in 1822?

6. What lighthouse east of Key Largo replaced the lightship *Florida*?

7. What lighthouse east of Sugarloaf Key was boarded by 24 Cuban refugees in 2016?

8. The Fresnal lens from what lighthouse is the on display at the Key West Lighthouse?

9. The Garden Key Light became the harbor light for what fort?

10. What Loggerhead Key lighthouse is the tallest lighthouse in the Keys?

QUIZ #27
ANSWERS

1. 88

2. She made statements against the Union.

3. It was decommissioned

4. Sand Key Light

5. Alligator Reef Light

6. Carysford Reef Light

7. American Shoals Light

8. Sombrero Key Light

9. Fort Jefferson

10. Dry Tortugas Light (157 feet)

NAME	SCORE	GRAND TOTAL

QUIZ #28
ARTISTS

1. What Cuban artist is known for his bas-relief woodcarvings of Key West street scenes?

2. What artist born in 1836 wintered in Key West and started his career as an illustrator for *Harper's Weekly*?

3. What ornithologist came to Key West looking for subjects to paint for his book *Birds of America*?

4. What Key West pop artist's cremains were passed on to friends in painted saltshakers?

5. What Key West artist did a series of small paintings called *Candy Bars* on metal shingles?

6. What junkyard rebel has a parade named after him? His sculptures are on display at the Fort East Martello Museum.

7. What marine artist painted the Whaling Wall on the Waterfront Brewery?

8. What local artist had a show called Nudes and Pets? He also founded the Zombie Bike Ride.

9. Whose larger-than-life sculptures can be found in front of the Custom House?

10. What local children's author was a cartoonist for *Playboy*?

QUIZ #28
ANSWERS

1. Mario Sanchez

2. Winslow Homer

3. John James Audubon

4. Captain Outrageous

5. Rick Worth

6. Stanley Papio

7. Wyland

8. Marky Pierson

9. Seward Johnson

10. Shel Silverstein

NAME	SCORE	GRAND TOTAL
_____	_____	_____
_____	_____	_____
_____	_____	_____
_____	_____	_____

QUIZ #29
TREES

1. What local tree is called the "tourist tree" because its trunk is red and peeling?

2. What tree has mammoth above ground roots and is also called the "tree of souls?" One is located in front of the courthouse.

3. The Monkey No Climb tree gets its name from what on its trunk?

4. What tree drops aerial prop roots that mature into trunks? A local resort is named after the tree.

5. What tree is sometimes called the "flame tree" for its flamboyant display of red flowers?

6. What tree with deep orange flowers did John James Audubon name for a local wrecker?

7. What trees make great honey, but are used primarily for shoreline ecosystem stabilization?

8. What group is appointed by the mayor to help regulate the removal of trees in Key West?

9. What Champion Tree does the Firehouse Museum hold a birthday party for each year?

10. What tree has wood so dense it doesn't float? It is said to have been used to create the Holy Grail.

QUIZ #29
ANSWERS

1. Gumbo Limbo

2. Kapok

3. Spikes

4. Banyan

5. Royal Poinciana

6. Geiger Tree

7. Mangroves

8. Tree Commission

9. Their Mamey tree

10. Lignum Vitae

NAME   **SCORE**   **GRAND TOTAL**

_____   _____   _____

_____   _____   _____

_____   _____   _____

_____   _____   _____

QUIZ #30
JIMMY BUFFETT

1. Who did Jimmy Buffett first come to Key West with in November of 1971?

2. What local grocery store does Jimmy buy chocolate milk from in the song *My Head Hurts, My Feet Stink and I Don't Love Jesus*?

3. Where does Jimmy go to get out of the heat in the song *Last Mango In Paris*?

4. In what song does Jimmy sing that all the good lookers seem to be Russian hookers from Key West to London town?

5. What song did Jimmy write about Key West renegade Phil Clark?

6. What is the name of Jimmy Buffett's Key West recording studio?

7. On what street is his recording studio located?

8. Jimmy's first apartment was located next to what bar?

9. In what bar did Jimmy play when he first came to Key West?

10. The City of Key West used the lyrics from a Buffett song in court while trying to prevent a tattoo shop from opening. What was the song?

QUIZ #30
ANSWERS

1. Jerry Jeff Walker

2. Fausto's

3. Captain Tony's

4. *A Lot To Drink About*

5. *A Pirate Looks at 40*

6. Shrimp Boat Sound

7. Lazy Way Lane

8. Louie's Backyard Afterdeck

9. The Chart Room

10. Margaritaville

NAME   **SCORE**   **GRAND TOTAL**

_____   _____   _____

_____   _____   _____

_____   _____   _____

_____   _____   _____

QUIZ #31
OTHER KEYS

1. What key is known as the "Diving Capital of the World?"

2. What "Village of Islands" name comes from the Spanish words meaning "island home?"

3. What key enforces a 35-mph speed limit at night to protect its population of Key Deer?

4. What city is home to Bonefish Tower? (At 143 feet., Bonefish Tower is the tallest building in the Keys.)

5. On what island can the landfill known as "Mt. Trashmore" be found?

6. What privately owned key is the southernmost point of land in the contiguous United States?

7. What keys, located about 25 miles northeast of Key West, were once home to a commercially operated breeding colony of rhesus monkeys?

8. What key's name is Spanish for "little mouth?" The Naval Air Station is located here.

9. What key is home to the only ghost town in the Florida Keys?

10. What is Wisteria Island often called by locals?

QUIZ #31
ANSWERS

1. Key Largo

2. Islamorada

3. Big Pine Key

4. Marathon

5. Stock Island

6. Ballast Key

7. Raccoon Key & Lois Key

8. Boca Chica

9. Indian Key

10. Christmas Tree Island

QUIZ #32
MILITARY

1. In what year did Lt. Commander Matthew C. Perry plant the US flag on Key West?

2. Matthew C. Perry arrived at Key West on a schooner. Name the schooner.

3. What was the nickname of the anti-piracy West Indies Squadron based out of Key West?

4. Where were crews from captured Confederate ships jailed in Key West during the Civil War?

5. The entire Atlantic Fleet, including the USS Maine, was moved to Key West prior to what war?

6. A submarine base and the Naval Air Station were added to the Navy's Key West footprint when the United States entered what war?

7. What happened after World War I that devastated the local economy?

8. What did the Navy start building in 1941 to provide water for the considerable number of troops they brought to Key West?

9. During what confrontation was the measurement "90 miles from Cuba" first introduced?

10. What military branch operates the Special Forces Underwater Operations School?

QUIZ #32
ANSWERS

1. 1822

2. Schooner Shark

3. The Mosquito Fleet

4. Fort Zachary Taylor

5. Spanish American War

6. World War I

7. The Navy Base closed.

8. A water pipeline from the mainland

9. The Cuban Missile Crisis

10. The U.S. Army

NAME   **SCORE**   **GRAND TOTAL**

_____   _____   _____

_____   _____   _____

_____   _____   _____

_____   _____   _____

QUIZ #33
MOVIES

1. Anna Magnani won an Oscar for her performance in what film based on a Tennessee Williams play and filmed, in part, next to his Key West home?

2. What 1959 film starring Cary Grant and Tony Curtis featured a pink submarine and was filmed around the Key West Naval Station?

3. What 1975 film starred Peter Fonda as a young man who opened a fishing business in Key West?

4. What 1986 film had Billy Crystal and Gregory Hines dreaming about opening a bar in Key West?

5. What 1989 James Bond film had Timothy Dalton skydive to a wedding at a Key West church?

6. In what 1995 movie starring Jamie Lee Curtis is the Seven Mile Bridge blown-up?

7. In what 1999 thriller does Cuba Gooding Jr.'s character retire to Key West to work on a book?

8. What 1997 movie starring Sandra Bullock filmed their evacuation scene in the Port of Key West?

9. What 1999 Mike Judge cult classic starring Ron Livingston filmed its final scene on Sunset Key?

10. What 1992 drama had Goldie Hawn working as a stripper in Key West while her son delivered fish?

QUIZ #33
ANSWERS

1. *The Rose Tattoo*

2. *Operation Petticoat*

3. *92 in the Shade*

4. *Running Scared*

5. *License to Kill*

6. *True Lies*

7. *A Murder of Crows*

8. *Speed 2: Cruise Control*

9. *Office Space*

10. *CrissCross*

NAME   **SCORE**   **GRAND TOTAL**

_____   _____   _____

_____   _____   _____

_____   _____   _____

_____   _____   _____

QUIZ #34

DUVAL STREET

1.   Who is Duval Street named after?

2.   How long is Duval Street?

3.   Why is Duval Street sometimes called "the longest street in the world?"

4.   What is a barhop spanning the length of Duval Street called?

5.   How many blocks long is Duval Street?

6.   What three-ton object conceived by Gregg McGrady spanned the length of Duval Street as part of the 2003 Pride Celebration?

7.   What is the tallest building on Duval Street?

8.   What year was the Oldest House on Duval Street built?

9.   Which artist sang, "Duval Street was rockin' / my eyes they started poppin'" on his *Havana Daydreamin'* album?

10. What annual run down Duval Street is part of the Conch Republic Independence Celebration?

QUIZ #34
ANSWERS

1. William Pope Duval, Florida's first territorial governor

2. Just over 1.25 miles

3. Because it stretches from the Gulf of Mexico to the Atlantic Ocean

4. The Duval Crawl

5. 14

6. The world's largest rainbow flag

7. The La Concha Hotel

8. 1829

9. Jimmy Buffett

10. The Duval Mile

NAME	SCORE	GRAND TOTAL
_____	_____	_____
_____	_____	_____
_____	_____	_____
_____	_____	_____

QUIZ #35
SEA CREATURES

1. What local sharks appear docile but are ranked fourth in documented shark bites against humans?

2. What aquatic mammals have their own playground in the shallow waters near Key West?

3. What aquatic mammals, sometimes referred to as "sea cows," can be found in the shallow waters near docks in Key West?

4. What local delicacy is named for its long pig-like snout?

5. What local sea creature is known for the barbed stingers on their tails?

6. What crustaceans are hunted in Key West each July when a mini-season permits their capture?

7. What is the dolphin fish also called so that people do not confuse it with dolphins like Flipper?

8. What colorful local fish eat coral from the reef and excrete it as sand?

9. What predator with sharp-edged fang-like teeth do snorkelers try to avoid? Heart sang about one.

10. What sea creatures have their own hospital in Marathon that rehabilitates them when they are injured?

QUIZ #35
ANSWERS

1. Nurse sharks

2. Atlantic Bottlenose Dolphins

3. Manatees

4. Hogfish

5. Stingrays

6. Spiny Lobster

7. Mahi-Mahi

8. Parrotfish

9. Barracuda

10. Sea Turtles

NAME   **SCORE**   **GRAND TOTAL**

_____   _____   _____

_____   _____   _____

_____   _____   _____

_____   _____   _____

QUIZ #36
BRIDGES

1. How many bridges connect Key West to the mainland?

2. What is the shortest bridge in the Florida Keys?

3. What is the longest bridge in the Florida Keys?

4. How long is the Seven Mile Bridge?

5. How many miles of the Overseas Highway is comprised of bridges?

6. Which Key West to Stock Island bridge hosts an annual "zero k" fun run?

7. What three Florida Keys bridges are listed on the National Register of Historic Places?

8. Several of the old railroad bridges in the Florida Keys been repurposed as what?

9. What marine artist selected the color "Belize Blue" for the median barriers on the Jewfish Creek Bridge?

10. What bridge has a tree named "Fred" growing on it?

QUIZ #36
ANSWERS

1. 42

2. Harris Gap Channel Bridge (37 feet)

3. Seven Mile Bridge

4. 6.79 miles

5. 18.8 miles

6. Cow Key Channel Bridge

7. Long Key Viaduct, Old Seven Mile Bridge, and Bahia Honda Rail Bridge

8. Fishing piers

9. Wyland

10. The Old Seven Mile Bridge

NAME   **SCORE**   **GRAND TOTAL**

_____   _____   _____

_____   _____   _____

_____   _____   _____

_____   _____   _____

QUIZ #37
FORT JEFFERSON

1. Fort Jefferson is the largest structure in the Americas made of what?

2. How many bricks are estimated to make up the fort?

3. On what key is Fort Jefferson located?

4. During the Civil War, President Lincoln substituted imprisonment on Fort Jefferson in lieu of execution for those found guilty of what crime?

5. What famous prisoner of Fort Jefferson is credited with writing "Whoso entereth here leaveth all hope behind" over the fort's dungeon?

6. What mosquito-borne epidemic plagued the fort in 1867?

7. In what 2006 novel by Max Brooks is Fort Jefferson used as a holdout by survivors of the zombie apocalypse?

8. What president upgraded the fort and surrounding area to national park status in 1992?

9. What was the name of the crocodile who spent 14 years at the fort?

10. How many people visit Fort Jefferson and the Dry Tortugas National Park each year?

QUIZ #37
ANSWERS

1. Brick

2. 16 million

3. Garden Key

4. Desertion

5. Samuel Mudd

6. Yellow fever

7. World War Z

8. President George H. W. Bush

9. Cleatus

10. 80,000

NAME	SCORE	GRAND TOTAL
_____	_____	_____
_____	_____	_____
_____	_____	_____
_____	_____	_____

QUIZ #38
SLOPPY JOE'S

1. Sloppy Joe officially opened his bar on December 5, 1933 when what was repealed?

2. What was Sloppy Joe's real name?

3. What was the name of Sloppy Joe's first bar?

4. What did Joe call his bar after a dance floor was added?

5. Who encouraged Joe to change his bar's name to "Sloppy Joe's?"

6. The name "Sloppy Joe's" came from a bar in another city where the ice leaked on the floor making it look sloppy. What was the city?

7. Sloppy Joe's moved across the street to its current location when the old landlord raised the rent from three dollars a week to what?

8. What business used to occupy the building on Duval and Greene Streets where Sloppy Joe's moved?

9. Hemingway call Sloppy Joe by what nickname?

10. A bat hangs on the wall at Sloppy Joe's. What 300-pound bartender used it to keep his customers in line?

QUIZ #38
ANSWERS

1. Prohibition or the 18ᵗʰ Amendment

2. Joe Russell

3. The Blind Pig

4. The Silver Slipper

5. Ernest Hemingway

6. Havana

7. Four dollars

8. The Victoria Restaurant

9. Josie Grunts

10. Big Skinner

NAME	SCORE	GRAND TOTAL
_____	_____	_____
_____	_____	_____
_____	_____	_____
_____	_____	_____

QUIZ #39
DIVING & WRECKS

1. Which collection of reefs is divided into Middle, Eastern, and Western by white sands?

2. What boat that was destined for Miami suspiciously sank near Key West and is home to a Jewfish named Elvis?

3. What island changes with weather patterns, making each dive unique, and has a 110-foot light tower?

4. What 187-foot buoy tender was seized during the Mariel boatlift before being sunk near Key West?

5. What 608-foot Cleveland Class cruiser is sunk off the coast of Cudjoe Key and rests in two parts?

6. What wrecked ship appeared in the 1957 film *Fire Down Below* and was named after a beer magnate before she was sunk as an artificial reef?

7. What ship was sunk seven miles south of Key West and was in the 1999 movie *Virus*?

8. In what "dry" dive area can an old sunken galleon barely be distinguished?

9. Who is Key West's local expert on sinking ships?

10. What destroyer escort boat that served in Normandy is now known as Alexander's Wreck?

QUIZ #39
ANSWERS

1. The Sambo Reefs

2. Joe's Tug

3. Sand Key

4. The Cayman Salvage Master

5. USS Wilkes-Barre

6. Adolphus Busch

7. The Vandenberg

8. The Eastern Dry Rocks

9. Joe Weatherby

10. USS Amesbury

NAME   **SCORE**   **GRAND TOTAL**

_____   _____   _____

_____   _____   _____

_____   _____   _____

_____   _____   _____

QUIZ #40
CAPTAIN TONY

1.   What is Captain Tony's last name?

2.   Where was Captain Tony born?

3.   After Captain Tony dropped out of school in 9th grade, what kind of liquor did he sell during prohibition?

4.   Captain Tony hitched a ride to Key West on what kind of truck?

5.   Captain Tony came to Key West with how much money?

6.   How many children did Captain Tony have?

7.   How many wives did Captain Tony have?

8.   What business did Captain Tony run for 35 years before opening his bar?

9.   What political position did Captain Tony win in 1989?

10. What ghost did Captain Tony claim to see when he was working the shrimp boats?

QUIZ #40
ANSWERS

1. Tarracino

2. Elizabeth, New Jersey

3. Whiskey

4. A milk truck

5. $18

6. 13

7. 4

8. Fishing boats

9. Mayor of Key West

10. The third man

NAME	SCORE	GRAND TOTAL
_____	_____	_____
_____	_____	_____
_____	_____	_____
_____	_____	_____

QUIZ #41
ANIMALS

1. What animals jump through hoops at sunset with Dominique LeFort?

2. What pink animals are the stars at the Key West Butterfly and Nature Conservatory?

3. What animals are often hated in Key West for their habit of eating flowering plants?

4. What animals were once prized in Key West for their fighting abilities?

5. Where are abandoned exotic animals often taken in Monroe County?

6. What big-eared animals roamed free at the Southernmost House and are still spotted in the surrounding neighborhood?

7. What reptile found in many Key West homes cannot blink, but can lose its tail in defense?

8. Monroe County spends as much as 14 million dollars a year to keep what insects under control?

9. What croakers first arrived in Key West on produce shipments from Cuba?

10. What local birds are known for their long beaks and large throat pouches?

QUIZ #41
ANSWERS

1. Cats

2. Flamingos

3. Iguanas

4. Roosters

5. Monroe County Sheriff's Animal Farm

6. Rabbits

7. Gecko

8. Mosquitoes

9. Cuban Tree Frogs

10. Pelicans

NAME	SCORE	GRAND TOTAL
_____	_____	_____
_____	_____	_____
_____	_____	_____
_____	_____	_____

QUIZ #42
RUM RUNNERS

1. Which Amendment made rum-running a lucrative trade in Key West?

2. Key West's proximity to what two countries made it a desirable location for importing illegal rum?

3. What kind of bar did Sloppy Joe Russell operate during prohibition?

4. Who tipped off illegal bar owners when federal agents were coming to town?

5. What nickname did Aeromarine Airways receive by flying "dry" residents of Key West to "wet" islands in the Caribbean?

6. What was the name of the favored watering hole in Havana during Prohibition?

7. What did a local undertaker use to conceal illegal rum he was taking to the mainland?

8. Marie Waite better known by what name when she ran a ruthless rum business that supplied Key West with rum from Havana?

9. In what nearby "Village of Islands" was the Rum Runner drink first created?

10. Who opened the first legal rum distillery in Key West?

QUIZ #42
ANSWERS

1. 18th Amendment (Prohibition)

2. Cuba & The Bahamas

3. A speakeasy

4. Railroad employees

5. The Highball Express

6. Sloppy Joe's

7. A casket

8. Spanish Marie

9. Islamorada

10. Paul Menta

NAME	SCORE	GRAND TOTAL
_____	_____	_____
_____	_____	_____
_____	_____	_____
_____	_____	_____

QUIZ #43
LGBT

1. What does LGBT stand for?

2. What Key West motto says that we are all unique and different and we are all of equal value?

3. What flag represents the LGBT community?

4. What memorial can be found at the entrance of the White Street Pier?

5. What Key West mayor was one of the first openly gay officials in the United States?

6. What notable gay resident said, "Maybe they weren't punks at all, but New York drama critics," after being mugged in Key West in 1979?

7. In what is drag queen Sushi dropped each New Year's Eve in Key West?

8. Key West's rainbow crosswalks are located at the intersection of what two streets?

9. What popular game is hosted by a drag queen each Sunday at 801 Bourbon?

10. What organization founded in 1978 supports and promotes LGBT businesses in Key West?

QUIZ #43
ANSWERS

1. Lesbian, gay, bisexual, transgender

2. One Human Family

3. The rainbow flag

4. AIDS Memorial

5. Richard Heyman

6. Tennessee Williams

7. A red shoe

8. Petronia & Duval

9. Bingo

10. The Key West Business Guild

NAME	SCORE	GRAND TOTAL
_____	_____	_____
_____	_____	_____
_____	_____	_____
_____	_____	_____

QUIZ #44
THE RAILROAD

1. Who made the dream of a railroad connecting Key West to the mainland a reality?

2. The planned construction of what sparked Henry Flagler's interest in extending his railroad to Key West's deep-water port?

3. Many people did not believe Flagler could complete the Over-Sea Railway. What did they call the project?

4. How many men were employed at the peak of construction of the Over-Sea Railway?

5. How many years of construction did it take to complete the Over-Sea Railway?

6. How much did the Over-Sea Railway project cost?

7. Once completed, the Over-Sea Railway was called the Eighth what?

8. What brought the Over-Sea Railway to an end in 1935?

9. How many miles of track were washed away in the Labor Day Hurricane of 1935?

10. How much did the State of Florida pay for the railroad's bridges and roadways so they could improve the Overseas Highway?

QUIZ #44
ANSWERS

1. Henry Flagler

2. The Panama Canal

3. Flagler's Folly

4. 4000

5. 11

6. More than $50 million

7. Wonder of the World

8. A hurricane

9. 40

10. $640,000

NAME	SCORE	GRAND TOTAL
_____	_____	_____
_____	_____	_____
_____	_____	_____
_____	_____	_____

QUIZ #45

FIRE

1. One of the first volunteer fire companies in the state of Florida was established in Key West in October of what year?

2. What did citizens do with the local fire truck after it failed to be useful during a fire in 1843?

3. When a large fire spread in 1859, what did Henry Mulrennon do to save neighboring houses?

4. With no fire department at the start of the Civil War, who took over fire responsibilities?

5. What caused the fire that interrupted the dedication of Key West's City Hall on July 4, 1876?

6. In the 1800s, fire engines in Key West were primarily used for what?

7. Why was Key West's fire engine in New York when the Great Fire of 1886 broke out?

8. Near which building did the Great Fire of 1886 start?

9. Fires used to be set intentionally to create a diversion when what was brought into Key West?

10. What well-known question is asked about a fire chief who mysteriously disappeared in 1975?

QUIZ #45
ANSWERS

1. 1834

2. Dumped it in the sea

3. Blew up his own house

4. The Union Army

5. A cannonball

6. Parades

7. For repairs

8. The San Carlos Institute

9. Drugs

10. Where is Bum Farto?

NAME	SCORE	GRAND TOTAL
_____	_____	_____
_____	_____	_____
_____	_____	_____
_____	_____	_____

QUIZ #46
TAGLINES

**PROVIDE THE POPULAR ADVERTISING TAGLINE
FOR EACH KEY WEST BUSINESS LISTED BELOW**

1. The Green Parrot?

2. Schooner Wharf Bar?

3. Angelina's Pizza?

4. Blue Heaven?

5. Old Town Trolley?

6. Sloppy Joe's?

7. Half Shell Raw Bar?

8. Fury Watersports?

9. Historic Tours of America?

10. Hog's Breath Saloon?

QUIZ #46
ANSWERS

1. A Sunny Place For Shady People

2. A Last Little Piece of Old Key West

3. Best Piece In Town

4. You Don't Have to Die to Get Here

5. Hop On, Hop Off

6. A Key West Tradition

7. Eat It Raw

8. Your Key West Story Starts Here

9. The Nation's Storyteller

10. Hog's Breath is Better Than No Breath at All

NAME	SCORE	GRAND TOTAL
_____	_____	_____
_____	_____	_____
_____	_____	_____
_____	_____	_____

QUIZ #47

CRIME

1. In what publication does the Key West Crime Report appear?

2. What website do locals use to look for mug shots of friends who have been arrested?

3. What item valued at $550,000 was stolen from a Key West museum in 2010?

4. What Shel Silverstein song has Shrimper Sam holding up a local tour vehicle?

5. What item was stolen from Key West in the aftermath of Hurricane Irma but later recovered in Tampa?

6. What is the most frequently stolen item in Key West?

7. What Key West resident was charged with "wantonly and maliciously destroying a grave and removing a body without authorization?"

8. Which Backstreet Boy was arrested in Key West after allegedly brawling outside a local bar?

9. The FBI declared Key West's police department a criminal enterprise in 1984. This became known by what name when 12 people were convicted?

10. What is the local slang for a floating bale of drugs?

QUIZ #47
ANSWERS

1. *The Key West Citizen*

2. www.keysso.net

3. A gold bar

4. *The Great Conch Train Robbery*

5. The "Welcome to Key West" sign

6. A bicycle

7. Carl Tanzler (Count Carl von Cosel)

8. Nick Carter

9. The Bubba Bust

10. Square grouper

NAME   **SCORE**   **GRAND TOTAL**

_____   _____   _____

_____   _____   _____

_____   _____   _____

_____   _____   _____

QUIZ #48
CUBA

1. Who founded the Cuban Revolutionary Party during his visits to Key West?

2. What is the name of Key West's Cuban heritage center, founded in 1871?

3. What Cuban leader ended his honeymoon in Key West in 1948?

4. What waterway lies between Key West and Cuba?

5. What mass emigration in 1980 brought boatloads of Cubans to Key West?

6. Can you see Cuba from Key West?

7. What is the locally made Cuban drink consisting of equal parts bold coffee and scalded milk?

8. What local sandwich is made with ham, roasted pork, Swiss cheese, pickles, mustard and salami on Cuban bread?

9. Cuban immigration to Key West was sparked in 1868 with the start of what war?

10. What was the name of the Cuban lottery played in Key West?

QUIZ #48
ANSWERS

1. Jose Marti

2. The San Carlos Institute

3. Fidel Castro

4. The Straits of Florida

5. The Mariel Boatlift

6. No

7. Café Con Leche

8. A Cuban Mix

9. The Ten Years' War

10. Bolita

NAME	SCORE	GRAND TOTAL
_____	_____	_____
_____	_____	_____
_____	_____	_____
_____	_____	_____

QUIZ #49
BUSINESS NAMES
FILL IN THE BLANK TO CPMPLETE THE LOCAL BUSINESS NAME

1.   _____ Plantation

2.   Eden _____

3.   Gone _____

4.   _____ Republic Seafood Co.

5.   _____ Mansion Inn

6.   Island _____ Story

7.   Southernmost _____ Hunt

8.   Sloan's _____ Hunt

9.   Phantom _____

10.   Chico's _____

QUIZ #49
ANSWERS

1. Coffee

2. House

3. Fishin'

4. Conch

5. Curry

6. Love

7. Scavenger

8. Ghost

9. Press

10. Cantina

NAME	SCORE	GRAND TOTAL
_____	_____	_____
_____	_____	_____
_____	_____	_____
_____	_____	_____

QUIZ #50
NOTABLE BUILDINGS
NAME THE NOTABLE BUILDING IN EACH PHOTOGRAPH
FROM THE MONROE COUNTY PUBLIC LIBRARY

What building was originally home to the island's postal service and district courts? The building was also the site of the inquiry into the sinking of the USS Maine.

2

What brick edifice built between 1890 and 1892
housed city offices as well as market stalls and fire
engines?

What hotel on Duval Street is the former home of cigar manufacturer Teodoro Perez and is named in part for the speeches Jose Marti gave from the home's balcony?

What Cuban heritage center was rebuilt in 1890 after the previous structure was destroyed in the Great Fire of 1886?

What house built by Judge Harris in 1897 claims to be one of the first homes in Key West with electricity?

6

What home built by Florida's first millionaire is also known as "the birthplace of Key lime pie?"

What 1901 building, built to support military training, was designed by T.F. Russell and became the initial campus of The Studios of Key West?

What concrete structure was built to protect the connections between the landlines and the 125-mile long underwater telegraph cable lines linking Key West and Havana?

What house was home to Florida's first Public Health Officer? It was built as a two-story house in 1839. A third story was added in 1870.

10

The founder of what black church intentionally maimed himself to avoid being sold back into slavery after purchasing his freedom?

QUIZ #50
ANSWERS

1. The Custom House

2. Old City Hall

3. La Te Da

4. San Carlos Institute

5. Southernmost House

6. Curry Mansion

7. Old Armory

8. The cable hut

9. Porter Mansion

10. Cornish Memorial AME Zion Church

NAME	SCORE	GRAND TOTAL
_____	_____	_____
_____	_____	_____
_____	_____	_____
_____	_____	_____

HOW DID YOU DO?

NAME

GRAND TOTAL

_____   _____

_____   _____

_____   _____

_____   _____

0-100 POINTS | VILLAGE IDIOT

It's time to face the fact that you are not top of your class when it comes to Key West knowledge. Don't worry. You can fix this by spending more time in Key West. Get out there and hit the museums, visit the bars and take a ride on the Conch Train. You will be an expert in no time.

100-200 POINTS | TOWN DRUNK

We're guessing you spend a little more time hitting the bottle than you do reading books about Key West. Don't sweat it. Key West would not be the same without you. Keep hanging with the locals and your knowledge will grow. In the mean time, enjoy your status as Key West's new town drunk.

200-300 POINTS | FRESHWATER CONCH

Give yourself a pat on the back. You have a pretty good knowledge of Key West that shows you have spent some time here getting to know the place. You know as much or more than someone who has lived here for seven years. Celebrate with a drink and enjoy your status as a Freshwater Conch.

300-400 | FULL-BLOWN CONCH

Nice work. The squirrel in your brain has been doing a fine job storing away nuggets of information about Key West. You know as much as or more than someone who was born and raised here. Try your shell of knowledge on for size. You are now a Full-Blown Conch.

400-450 | KEY WEST BUBBA

Damn you are good. Not only are you smarter about Key West than most people taking these quizzes, you are smarter than most people in Key West, including those that were born here. You have blown the Conch status away. You are a dialed in Bubba.

450-500 | ISLAND GENIUS

You are a genius. Key West flows through your veins. It oozes from your pores. If "Key West Expert" was an entry in the dictionary, it would be accompanied by a photograph of you. You are so damn good you probably even spotted a few mistakes in the book. Keep them to yourself and bask in the glow that comes from being an Island Genius.

ALSO BY DAVID L. SLOAN

QUIT YOUR JOB & MOVE TO KEY WEST

GHOSTS OF KEY WEST

HAUNTED KEY WEST

ROBERT THE HAUNTED DOLL

KEY WEST 101

THE KEY WEST HANGOVER SURVIVAL GUIDE

THE KEY WEST BUCKET LIST

THE FLORIDA KEYS BUCKET LIST

A LOCAL'S GUIDE TO BLOODLINE

A LOCAL'S GUIDE TO BLOODLINE 2

THE KEY WEST KEY LIME PIE COOKBOOK

ROOSTERS ARE ASSHOLES

IGUANAS ARE ASSHOLES

THE LOST DIARY OF COUNT VON COSEL

THE HAVANA BUCKET LIST

THE HEMINGWAY FBI FILES

TUTU, THE ALMOST HEMINGWAY CAT

DAVID L SLOAN

David Sloan moved to the Florida Keys in 1996. He is the author of 19 books including Quit Your Job and Move to Key West and The Key West Bucket List. Sloan also runs the popular ghost tour and ghost hunt company, Haunted Key West, and co-produces the Key Lime Festival and the Zero K Cow Key Channel Bridge Run.

Contact david@phantompress.com

Made in United States
Cleveland, OH
30 November 2024

11103822R00069